THIS JOURNAL BELONGS TO:

Welcome to Your Grief Journal

Losing someone we care about is one of the hardest things we can go through. This journal is here to help you as you work through your feelings, memories, and experiences with grief. There's no right or wrong way to grieve, and everyone's journey looks a little different.

This journal is a safe space for you to express how you feel, think about your loved one, and learn ways to take care of yourself along the way. You'll find questions, activities, and helpful tools to guide you as you move through the different stages of grief. Take your time, and remember that it's okay to feel sad, confused, or even angry. It's also okay to find moments of joy and comfort in your memories.

As you go through this journal, be gentle with yourself. You're not expected to have all the answers or feel better right away, but step by step, you'll find ways to manage your emotions and start healing. This is your space to reflect, to remember, and to take care of your heart.

ALL ABOUT ME

NAME _________________   NICKNAME _________________

STAR SIGN _________________   D.O.B _________________

FAVOURITE FOODS

____
____
____

FAVOURITE SONGS

____
____
____

IF I WON A MILLION DOLLARS, WHAT WOULD I DO WITH IT?

WORDS THAT DESCRIBE ME

____
____
____

IN MY SPARE TIME I LIKE TO

____
____
____

A QUOTE THAT INSPIRES ME IS

ALL ABOUT MY LOVED ONE

My favorite memory with them was...

Things that remind me of them...

They loved doing..

ALL ABOUT MY LOVED ONE

Their favorite saying was....

My loved one was good at...

The thing that I admire most about them is...

ALL ABOUT MY LOVED ONE

If they saw me right now they would say to me...

If I saw them right now I would say to them...

REFLECTION

STAGES OF GRIEF

Gaining an understanding of the various stages of grief can provide you with more insight and make the process a little easier. Keep in mind that everyone experiences grief in their own way, and not everyone will go through each stage in the same sequence.

SHOCK AND DENIAL

Even if you anticipated the loss of a loved one, their passing can still come as a shock. This stage serves as emotional protection, helping to shield you from the overwhelming pain and intensity of the situation. You might feel numb or disconnected, and while you're aware that the loss has occurred, it may feel unreal, as though it hasn't truly happened yet.

GUILT

People may irrationally blame themselves for events they had no control over. Guilt leads to self-punishment and traps us in focusing on the past.

ANGER

Your pain might manifest as anger, irritability, rage, bitterness, anxiety, impatience, or even lashing out and placing unwarranted blame. In this stage, you begin to recognize that certain things have changed, which often leads to frustration or anger directed toward your new reality.

BARGAINING

During this stage, people often cling to hope despite their intense pain. You may find yourself feeling like you would do anything or make any sacrifice to have your loved one back.

DEPRESSION

Feeling depressed is a normal and appropriate reaction during the grieving process. In this stage, you begin to confront the reality that your loved one is truly gone and fully grasp the magnitude of your loss. It's common to experience feelings of emptiness, despair, and isolation during this time.

ACCEPTANCE

Acceptance doesn't mean you feel okay or right about the loss; rather, it's about recognizing that the new reality cannot be altered. It involves embracing the present, both the good and the bad, in order to move forward and shape the future.

STAGES OF GRIEF

Consider writing down your thoughts, feelings, and experiences as you navigate through the stages of grief. Keep in mind that everyone goes through these stages differently, and they may not follow a set order. There is no right or wrong way to grieve.

SHOCK AND DENIAL

PAIN AND GUILT

ANGER

BARGAINING

DEPRESSION

ACCEPTANCE

Common symptoms
OF GRIEF

Everyone experiences grief in their own unique way. Below are some common symptoms of grief that may affect your thoughts, behavior, and body. Check any that resonate with your experience.

PHYSICAL

- ☐ MUSCLE PAINS
- ☐ NAUSEOUS
- ☐ HEADACHES
- ☐ BACKACHES
- ☐ BLOATING
- ☐ STOMACH PAINS
- ☐ RUN DOWN
- ☐ WEIGHT LOSS
- ☐ CHEST PAIN

SOCIAL

- ☐ OVERWHELMED
- ☐ HOPELESS
- ☐ EMPTY
- ☐ NUMB
- ☐ FRUSTRATED
- ☐ ANGRY
- ☐ IRRITABLE
- ☐ SADNESS
- ☐ GUILT

BEHAVIOR

- ☐ WITHDRAWAL
- ☐ BAD HYGIENE
- ☐ SLEEP DISTURBANCES
- ☐ CHANGES IN PERSONAL
- ☐ APPEARANCE
- ☐ NOT CALLING OR TEXTING PEOPLE BACK
- ☐ NOT DOING THINGS THAT YOU ONCE ENJOYED
- ☐ LACK OF EXERCISE

OTHER

- ☐ _______________________
- ☐ _______________________
- ☐ _______________________
- ☐ _______________________
- ☐ _______________________
- ☐ _______________________
- ☐ _______________________
- ☐ _______________________
- ☐ _______________________
- ☐ _______________________

MEMORY BOX

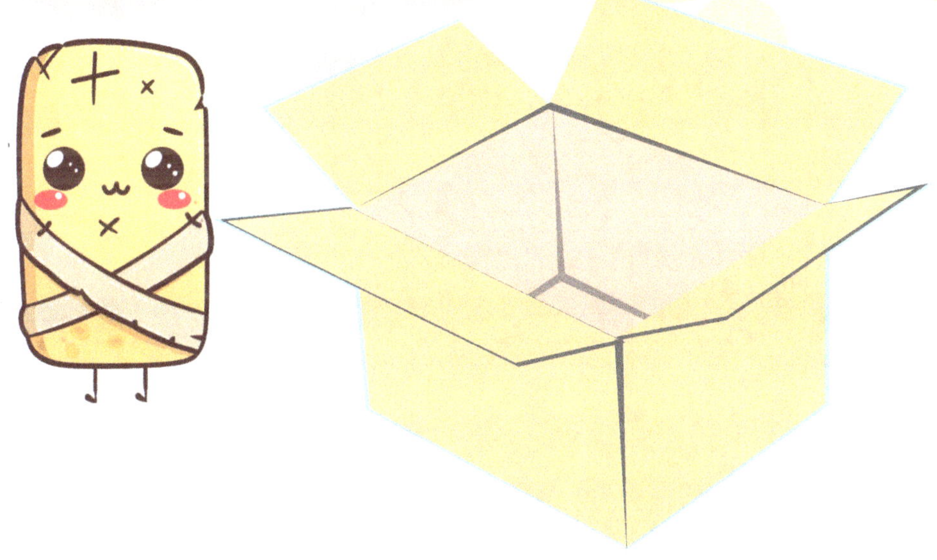

GROWING AROUND GRIEF

The "growing around grief" model, developed by grief counselor Lois Tonkin, suggests that grief itself doesn't diminish over time. Instead, your life expands around it. As you encounter new experiences and continue living, these moments gradually form around the grief. While the loss remains a part of you, you also begin to move forward, creating space for growth beyond the grief.

CHANGING SEASONS

Change is an unavoidable part of life. Whether anticipated or surprising, it accompanies us from birth to death, affecting everything from seasons and age to homes and friendships. Like it or not, change surrounds us every day. Sadly, grief is also a part of these inevitable changes that life brings.

SUMMER

AUTUMN

WINTER

SPRING

CHANGING AGES

Our age is constantly changing; whether we embrace it or not, we are continuously growing and getting older.

Can you create a drawing of yourself at different ages? Imagine how you might look and what activities you would enjoy during each stage of life.

BABY

NOW

TEENAGER

ADULT

CIRCLE OF CONTROL

Many aspects of life are beyond our control. It's important to concentrate your time and energy on what you can influence and release the things you cannot.

Could you try adding more examples below?

Things I can NOT control

- So I can let Go of these things

What other people think

What other people believe

Other people's actions

The weather

Things I can control

- So I will focus on these things

Who I spend time with

My Boundaries

My thoughts

My values and beliefs

MY SUPPORT NETWORK

HAVING PEOPLE IN YOUR LIFE WHOM YOU CAN TALK ABOUT YOUR FEELINGS IS IMPORTANT.

If you went to space, who would you feel comfortable taking?

CIRCLE OF CONTROL

"I ENJOYED RETURNING TO SCHOOL AND SEEING MY FRIENDS; I KNOW T HAT MY DAD WOULD WANT ME TO CONTINUE LIVING MY LIFE AND BE HAPPY."

"I STILL HAVE DAYS WHEN I FEEL UPSET. SOMETIMES I HEAR THEIR FAVORITE SONG, AND IT MAKES ME SAD. BUT WITH TIME, IT STARTS TO GET EASIER."

"I FOUND IT HELPFUL TO TALK TO MY FRIENDS ABOUT MY FEELINGS. IN THE BEGINNING, THEY FELT A BIT AWKWARD, BUT I REASSURED THEM THAT IT WAS OKAY TO ASK ME HOW I WAS DOING."

"MY SISTER'S DEATH CAME AS A COMPLETE SHOCK AND WAS UNEXPECTED, BUT WE ARE A RESILIENT FAMILY."

The Tasks OF GRIEF

Many people frequently ask, "How do I grieve?" Navigating the grieving process can be difficult, and many individuals attempt to suppress their emotions in an effort to feel better. However, research consistently indicates that this approach can be harmful. The T.E.A.R model views grief not as a set of emotions or stages to go through, but rather as tasks to be completed and worked through.

T

TO ACCEPT THE REALITY OF YOUR LOSS

Have you accepted the loss of your loved one? How could you accept your loss?

E

EXPERIENCE THE PAIN OF YOUR LOSS

How do experience your loss? Where can you feel pain within your body?

A

ADJUST TO YOUR NEW ENVIRONMENT

What adjustments do you need to make to your new environment?

R

REINVEST IN YOUR NEW REALITY

How can you find a way to remember your loved one, while moving forward in your life.?

GRATITUDE

When you express gratitude, you acknowledge your appreciation for something, allowing you to cherish the memories and what remains. For instance, even though you may feel deep sadness over losing someone, you might still feel thankful for the time you shared with them or for the things you still hold onto.

A memory with my loved one that I am grateful for is...

Things about me that I am grateful for...

Things that I have learnt this year and grateful for are...

My loved one would be most grateful for...

I am grateful for my life because?

GRIEF AND MY BODY

Each person's body reacts to grief differently, but there are some common physical symptoms.

Close your eyes and take a deep breath in through your nose, then slowly exhale through your mouth. Starting from the top of your head, focus on how each part of your body feels. Gradually work your way down, paying attention to any sensations, all the way to your toes. Can you identify any areas of discomfort on the body below?

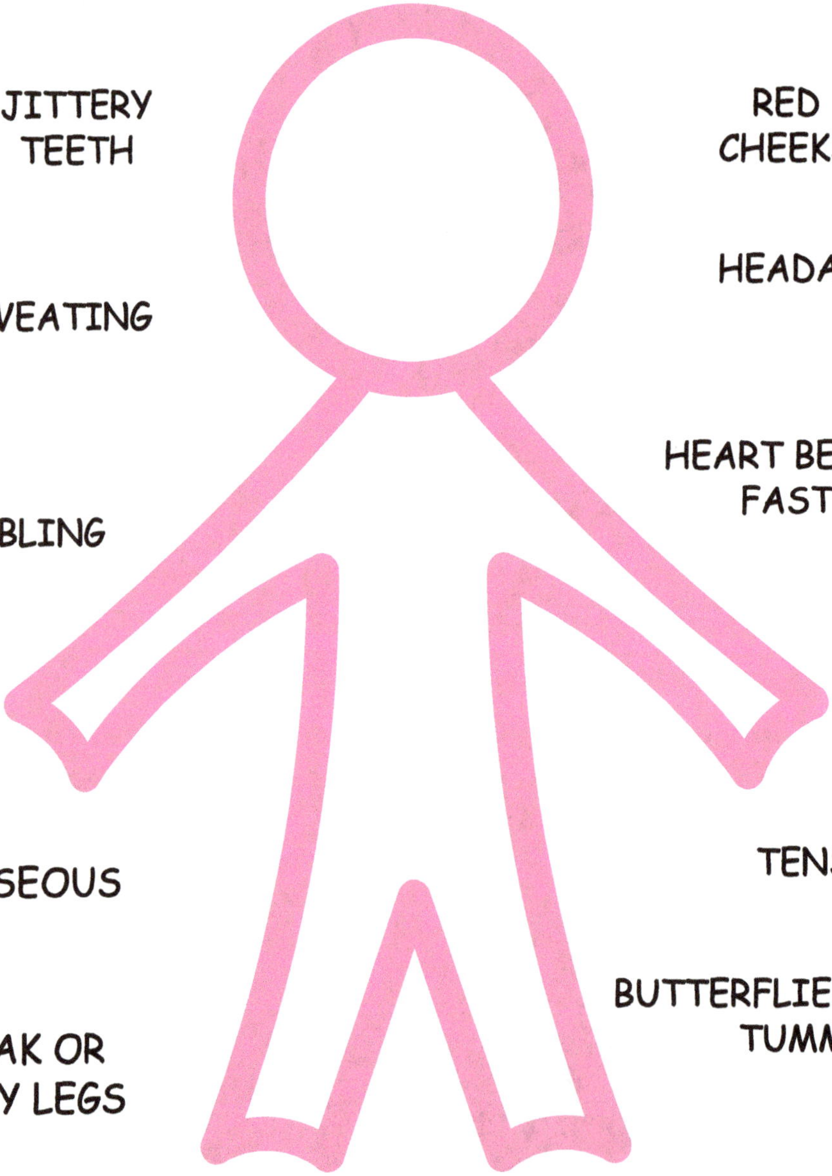

JITTERY TEETH

RED CHEEKS

HEADACHE

SWEATING

HEART BEATS FAST

TREMBLING

NAUSEOUS

TENSE

BUTTERFLIES IN THE TUMMY

WEAK OR JELLY LEGS

CHEST PAIN

CLENCHED FISTS

THAT TIME OF THE YEAR

Grief is often complex, and certain times of the year can make it feel even more overwhelming. This might be the anniversary of their passing, their birthday, or another significant date that holds special meaning for you.When these moments arrive, it's natural to find them more difficult than usual, and that's perfectly okay. However, there are ways you can manage and cope with these challenging periods.

TALK ABOUT IT

Talking about your loved one can help you through the grieving process. List the people that you couldtalk to.

VISIT YOUR LOVED ONE

Is there a place where you could visit your loved one? Maybe it is a place where they were laid to rest,and you could take some flowers and talk to them.

DO SOMEHTING SPECIAL THAT MAKES YOU FEEL CONNECTED TO THEM

Is there something that you could do that makes you feel connected to your Loved one? Maybe it's listeningto their favorite music, watching their favorite movie, or making their favorite food.

WRITE A LETTER

Write a letter to your loved one, tell them about what you have been up to in your life, and list yourachievements and things you are proud of. Then, tell them how you feel.
List three things that you would like to write in your letter.

DO SOMETHING THAT MAKES YOU FEEL HAPPY

What do you like to do that makes you feel happy, safe, and calm? Doing something that you enjoy will help you through the grief.

MY HEART MAP

Fill each area with a color that represents a particular emotion, place, or memory that reminds you of your loved one. Let yourself be open to all the big and small things that come to mind.

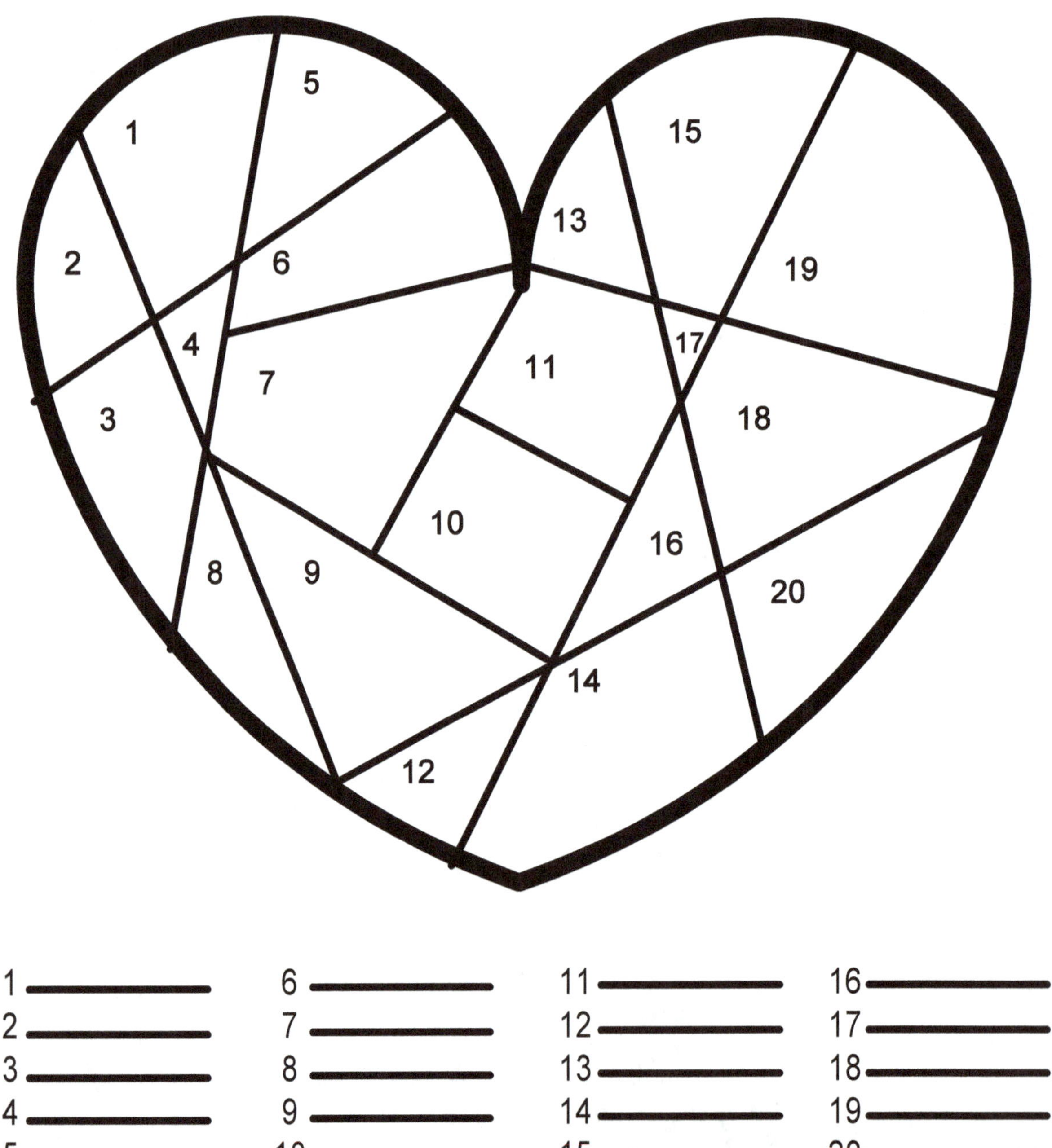

1 _______
2 _______
3 _______
4 _______
5 _______

6 _______
7 _______
8 _______
9 _______
10 _______

11 _______
12 _______
13 _______
14 _______
15 _______

16 _______
17 _______
18 _______
19 _______
20 _______

THAT TIME OF THE YEAR

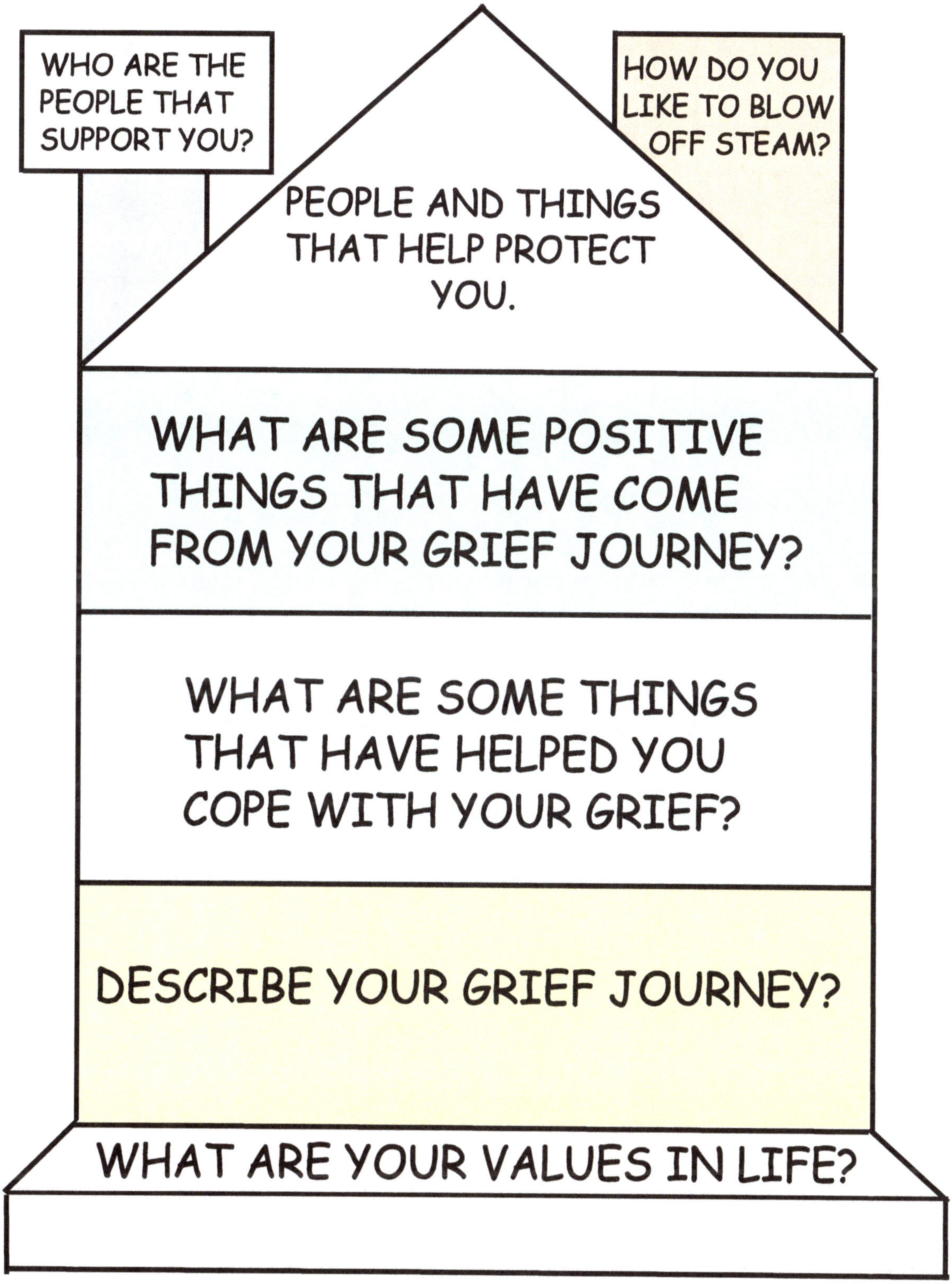

MY GRIEF HOUSE

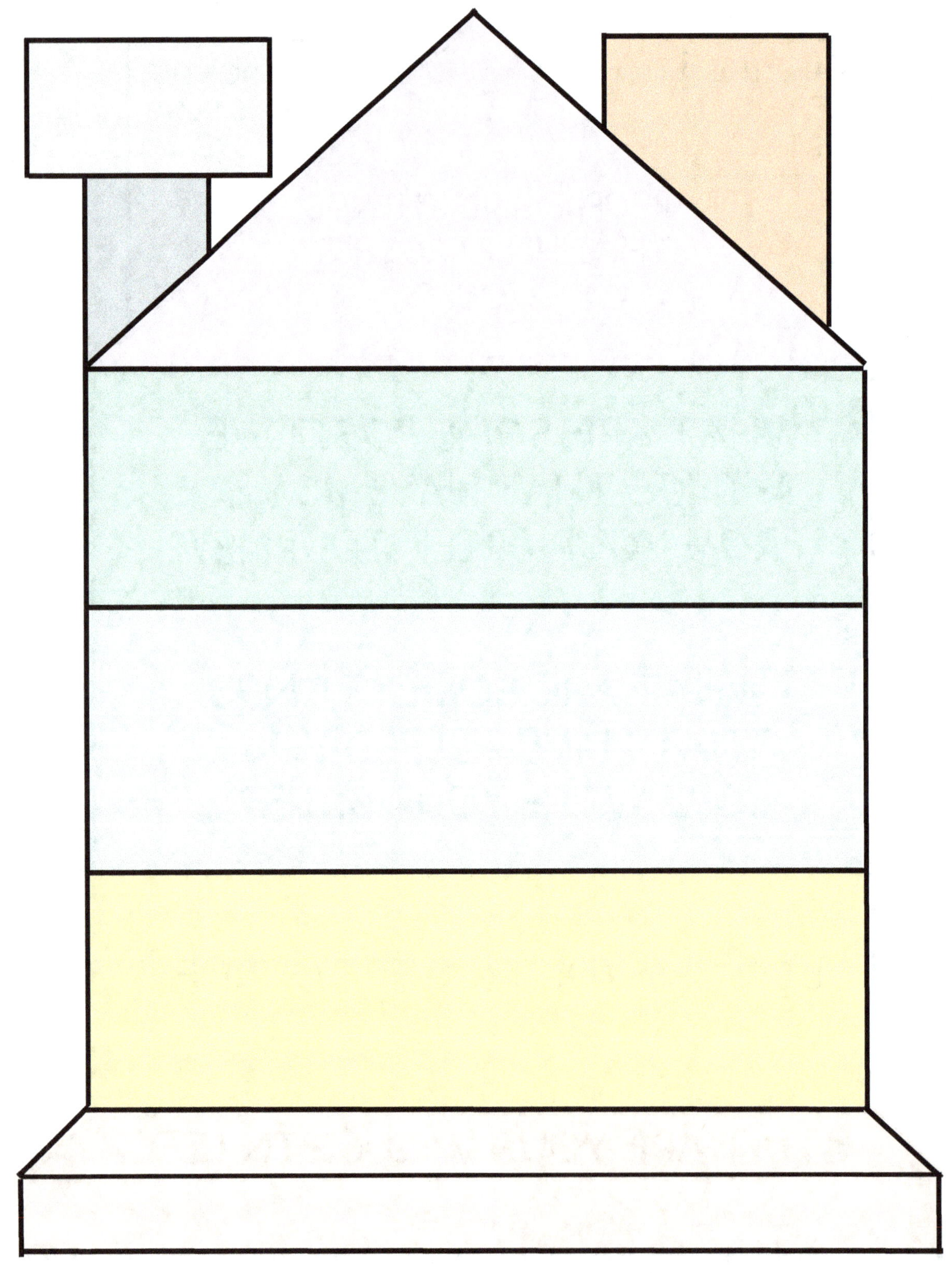

MY GRIEF RESPONSE

Have you been noticing any of these symptoms since the loss of your loved one?
Check the box that relates to you and note how frequently they occur.

- [ ] CHANGE IN APPETITE
- [ ] TIGHTNESS IN CHEST
- [ ] ANXIETY OR FEAR
- [ ] DIFFICULTY SLEEPING
- [ ] UNMOTIVATED
- [ ] CRYING
- [ ] ANGRY - OUTBURSTS
- [ ] MOODSWINGS
- [ ] SOCIAL WITHDRAWAL
- [ ] ENGAGING IN DANGEROUS ACTIVITIES
- [ ] BLAMING MYSELF
- [ ] POOR CONCENTRATION
- [ ] UNABLE TO STOP THOUGHTS
- [ ] LONLINESS
- [ ] SADNESS - DEPRESSION
- [ ] NIGHTMARES
- [ ] UNMOTIVATED - LOW ENERGY
- [ ] DAYTIME SLEEPINESS
- [ ] SHOCK
- [ ] NAUSEOUS
- [ ] DENIAL
- [ ] NUMBNESS
- [ ] QUESTIONING LIFE AND BELIEFS
- [ ] HOPELESS
- [ ] FEAR OF DEATH

WHAT I NEED

What do I need from my family?

What do I need from my friends?

What do I need from others?

My letter to YOU

When a loved one passes away, you might feel like there are still things left unsaid. Maybe you didn't get the opportunity, or you weren't sure how to express those feelings at the time. Now, you have the chance to write a letter to your loved one and share what's on your heart.

My letter to YOU

My letter to YOU

My letter to YOU

My letter to **YOU**

Tangled Ball
OF GRIEF

Grief can feel like a tangled ball of emotions. These feelings often ebb and flow, and you may find yourself experiencing multiple emotions all at once.

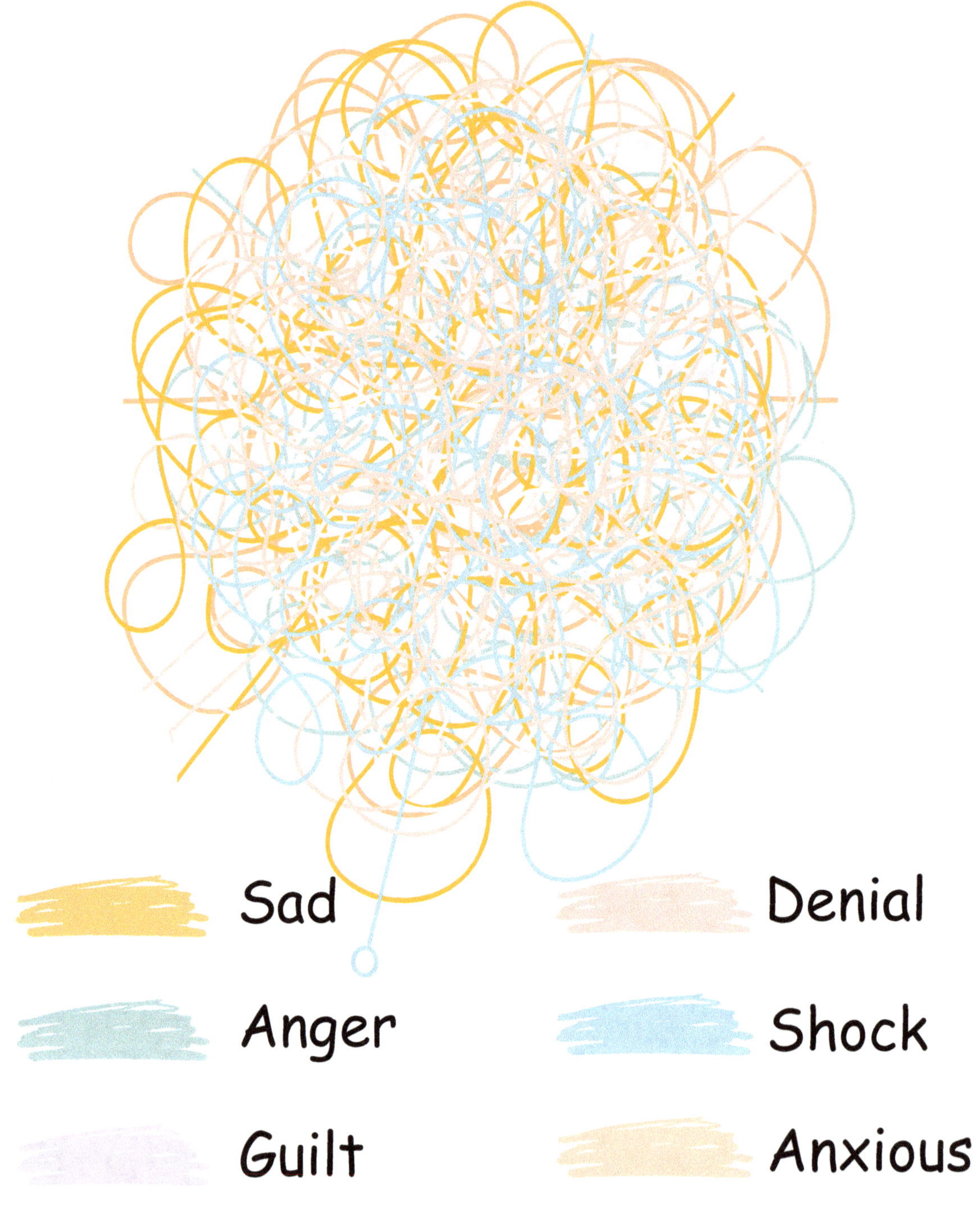

EMOTIONS WHEEL

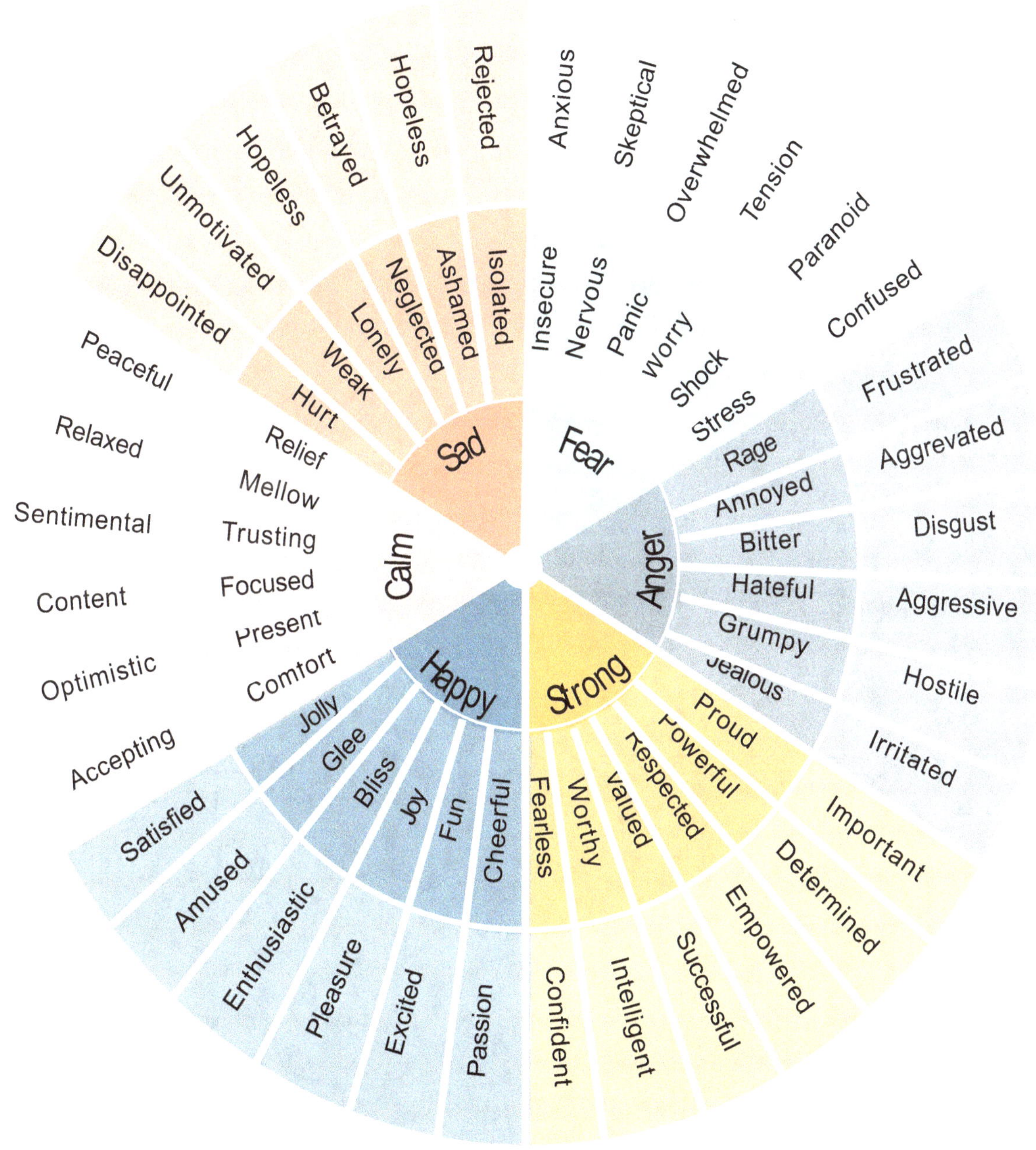

MY GRIEF ICEBERG

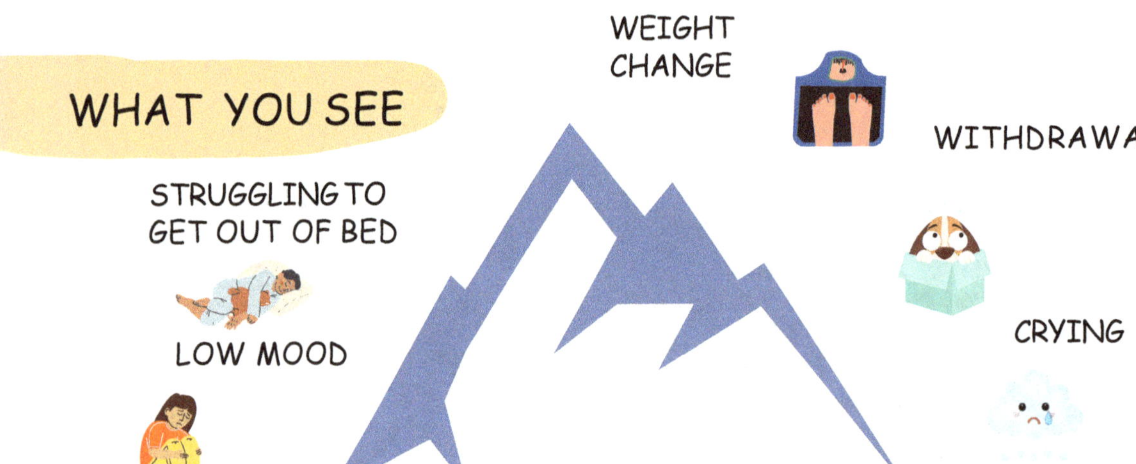

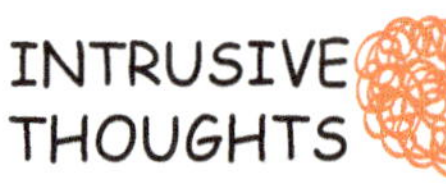

MY GRIEF ICEBERG

The iceberg theory illustrates the concept that while grief may be visible on the outside, many other emotions remain concealed beneath the surface. Like an iceberg, the true depth of what lies beneath is not immediately apparent. The behavior you observe is just "the tip of the iceberg," while the emotional, social, and other underlying factors remain hidden, influencing that outward behavior.

WHAT YOU SEE

WHAT YOU DON'T SEE

FILL IN YOUR OWN ICEBERG

Sleepiness	Suicidal thoughts	Memory problems	Crying	Numb
Fatigued	Hopeless	Low appetite	Giving up	Grief
Low energy	Loneliness	Big appetite	Poor hygiene	Anger
Lack of concentration	Shame	Withdrawal	Low confidence	Insomnia
Self harm	Guilt	Addiction	Anxiety	Tremors

COPING SKILLS

When we experience intense emotions such as frustration, excitement, anger, anxiety, or embarrassment, we might act in unpredictable or irrational ways, which can leave us feeling uncomfortable or behaving in ways we're not proud of.

During these moments, it can be difficult to think clearly and determine the best course of action to help calm ourselves. This is where coping skills come in.

Coping skills are techniques that assist in calming down, managing emotions, and regulating your responses to situations around you. They can be used when you're feeling anxious, uneasy, or worried to help you navigate through challenging times.

These strategies are designed to reduce physical symptoms of distress and help you regain clarity of thought. Everyone has a unique set of coping skills that work best for them, and yours may differ from others - and that's perfectly okay. The goal is to find what helps you manage your thoughts, emotions, and actions in a more positive and constructive way.

This activity highlights common coping strategies for most people, but over time, you'll discover which ones work best for you and might even come up with your own ideas to add to the list.

MY COPING SKILLS TRACKER - DIARY

Keep track of the coping strategies that are most effective in different situations; you may begin to notice a pattern. Once you've identified techniques that work well, you can brainstorm additional coping strategies to try in the future.

WHAT HAPPENED	BEHAVIOR	COPING STRATEGY USED	RESULT

MY COPING SKILLS TRACKER - DIARY VOL 2

Keep a log of the coping techniques that prove effective in various scenarios; over time, you might recognize recurring patterns. Once you find the strategies that help you, consider exploring and brainstorming new ones to incorporate as well.

WHAT HAPPENED	BEHAVIOR	COPING STRATEGY USED	RESULT

HOW AM I FEELING?

Calm

Happy

Worried

Excited

Frustrated

Scared

Sad

Shy

Angry

Nervous

Tired

Loving

Play sport

Playing sport help stake your mind off the things that were bothering you. It is also so mething fun to do.

Take deep breaths

Breathe slowly in through your nose, and then slowly out through your mouth.

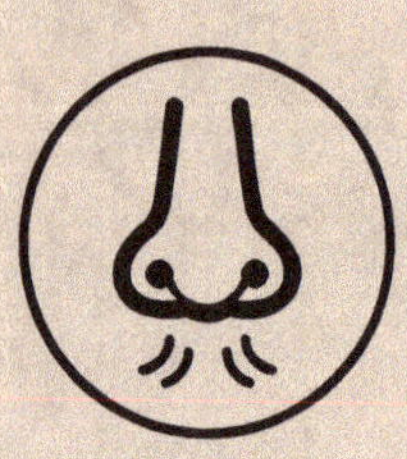

Do some colouring in or drawing

Grab a piece of paper and try drawing a picture of your favorite memory.

Count to10

Count to 10 slowly. When you have finished you can then count back wards from 10 to1

Eat some healthy food

Eating healthy food is good for your body and brain.

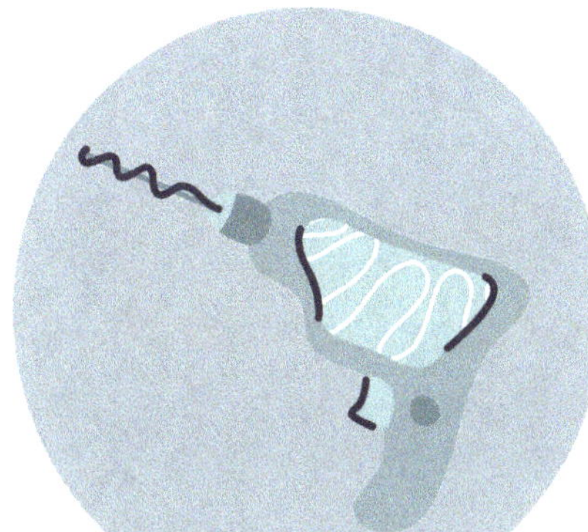

Listen to my favourite music

Make aplay list with all your favourite songs on it.

Have a warm bath

Take time out by having a nice warm bath. This will help you feel calm and relaxed.

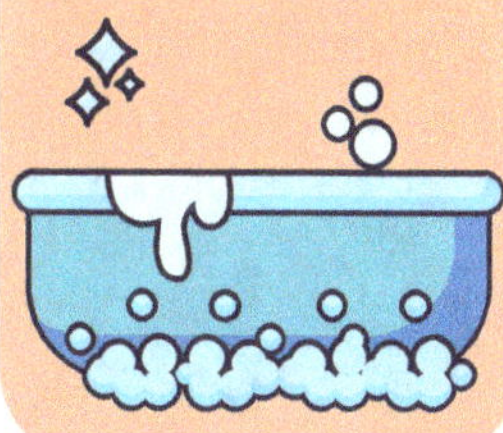

Do some stretching

When you get upset your muscles start to tense up. Stretching your body will help you to feel better.

Go for a bike ride

Try going for a bike ride. Doing exercise and getting fresh air is a great way to feel better.

Talk to myself nicely

Write down or say all the things that you like about yourself.

Read
a book

Find a
quiet place
and read
your
favourite
book.

Think of
my favourite
memories

Try
switching
your
thoughts in
your mind.
You can do
this by
thinking
about your
favourite
memory

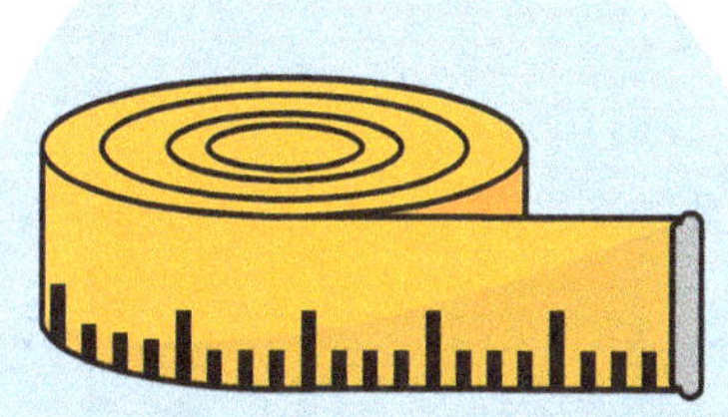

Go for
a run

Go for
a run or
participate
in some
exercise.
This will
help you
to feel calm
and happy.

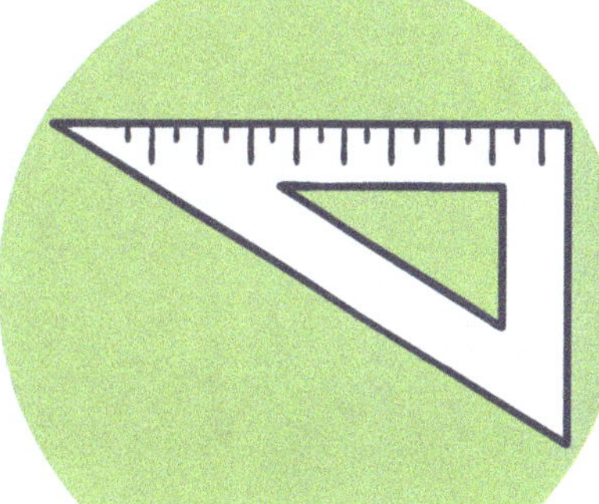

Write in
your
journal.

Write in
your
journal.
Expressing
your
feelings will
help you
feel
better
again.

THE GRIEF WHIRLPOOL

THE GRIEF WHIRLPOOL

"Bereavement is what happens to you, grief is how you feel, and mourning is how you respond."

Bereavement can be compared to a wound, while grief represents the pain caused by that wound. Some wounds are deeper than others, and healing can take time, but if we tend to that wound with care, eventually it will heal, leaving behind a scar.

Mourning is the action we take during this healing journey, and the coping strategies along with self-care practices play a crucial role in helping your wound heal over time.

What is the 'Grief Whirlpool'?

After losing a loved one, it's common to experience a wide range of emotions such as shock, numbness, anger, and denial. Sometimes, the situation may feel too overwhelming or complicated to process, and your emotions might not work as they should. This can lead to your feelings getting caught in a whirlwind, causing you to face some of the most painful and devastating emotions.

An emotional whirlpool happens when different grief-related emotions become entangled in a dysfunctional way, trapping energy and intensifying those feelings until they become overwhelming. Being stuck in this emotional whirlpool can make it hard to escape, and you may find yourself going in circles, relying on unhealthy coping mechanisms that offer temporary relief but keep you trapped in the cycle.

However, if you manage to free yourself from this emotional spiral, much like a river continues to flow downstream, your emotions will eventually reorganize themselves, leading to mourning, acceptance, love, and a renewed sense of hope for the future.

THE GRIEF WHIRLPOOL

The River of Life

Write about your loved one. What type of person were they? What is your favorite memory of them?

Shock, denial and numbness

Write about your feelings when you lost your loved one. What was your initial expereince?

'The Whirlpool'

Are you caught up in a whirlpool of emotions that you haven't dealt with? Have you created a vicious cycle of using unhealthy coping skills?

THE GRIEF WHIRLPOOL

The Rocks

What pain and symptoms in your body do you feel when you experience your grief?

Mourning and Acceptance

What healthy coping skills can you use to help you through your mourning process?

Hope

What brings you hope about the future? What do you have to look forward to again?

HEALTHY COPING SKILLS

EAT 3 HEALTHY MEALS	HAVE A SOCIAL MEDIA DETOX
7+ HOURS OF SLEEP	ASK FOR A HUG
DRINK FRESH WATER	SPEND TIME WITH FAMILY
GET FRESH AIR	DO A HOBBY
PRACTICE MINDFULNESS	WRITE IN YOUR JOURNAL
WRITE DOWN 3 THINGS YOU ARE GRATEFUL FOR	SAY 5 THINGS YOU LOVE ABOUT YOURSELF
BRUSH YOUR TEETH	DO SOME EXERCISE
HAVE A WARM SHOWER	WASH YOUR HAIR
MAKE YOUR BED	HAVE A CUP OF TEA
READ A BOOK	DO NOTHING- ENJOY THE PEACE
LISTEN TO MUSIC	TRY SOMETHING NEW
SPEND TIME WITH FRIENDS	DO SOME COLORING IN
DECLUTTER A SMALL SPACE	MAKE YOUR FAVORITE FOOD
WRITE A GOODBYE LETTER	SPEND TIME IN NATURE
CONNECT WITH NEW PEOPLE	READ A FUNNY BOOK

SELF-CARE WHEEL

Self-care is a crucial survival tool during the grieving process. It involves practices or activities that we engage in regularly to alleviate stress and support our physical and mental well-being. Essentially, self-care is anything you do for yourself that promotes a sense of comfort and care.

This self-care wheel outlines different aspects of self-care, providing a straightforward action plan to help manage grief and stress while promoting a more balanced and fulfilling daily life.

Sleep

There is a close connection between sleep and mental health as inadequate sleep is associated with an increase of frequent mental distress. A good night's sleep helps foster both mental and emotional resilience. It is recommended that healthy adults need between 7 and 9 hours of sleep per night.

Nutrition /exercise

Exercise helps strengthen ones mental health. Exercise releases chemicals like endorphins and serotonin that improve your mood. Additionally, better quality diets are consistently associated with reduced depression risk

Social interaction

Social connection is a fantastic resource for your self-care. Social self-care means having loving, healthy, and supportive relationships. It makes us feel appreciated and gives us a sense of belonging.

SELF-CARE

Hobbies/ Interests

Spending time doing something that you enjoy such as painting, art, knitting, crochet or any activity that brings you pleasure will help increase your moods and lower your stress levels.

Gratitude

Gratitude is a highly effective resource for self-care. Practicing gratitude is one way we can take time to reflect on the things that we value and appreciate. Research indicates that by practicing gratitude daily you can increase your mental well being.

Boundaries

Setting personal boundaries is an important part of your own self care and can help you honour and respect your own emotional, psychological and physical needs.

GRIEF QUESTION CARDS

These cards have questions that can help you think about your feelings after losing someone. Each card is meant to help you reflect on your emotions, memories, and experiences with grief. Take your time as you go through the cards, and answer them at your own pace, allowing yourself to feel and understand how each question connects to your experiences.

Tell me
about the
person you
are grieving?

Has anything
surprised you
since the
passing of your
loved one?

Do you like
to talk about
your loved
one?

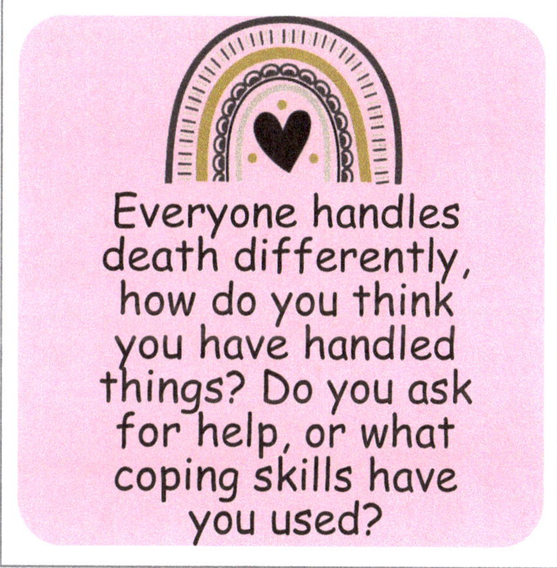

Everyone handles
death differently,
how do you think
you have handled
things? Do you ask
for help, or what
coping skills have
you used?

What time
of the day
do you
find the
hardest?

Do you like
to reminisce about
your loved one by
sharing stories,
listening to music
or looking at
photos?

Have you had
to change your
plans for
the future?

Do you have
any regrets?
if so,how do
you think
you can
overcome
them?

What do you
miss the
most?

How are you
feeling right
now?

Is there
anything, anyone
or any places
that you have
been avoiding?

How can you
continue to
honour your
loved one?

Do you think
grief gets
easier
with time?

Is there a song
that reminds
you of your
loved one?

Do you have
anyother friends
that have
experienced
grief?

Emotions from
grief can
appear at
random times,
why do you
think
that is?

Has your
grief
changed
you?

Grief often
makes people
appreciate
their own life,
why do you
think thatis?

Do you think you have accepted the death of your loved one?

What do you need the most help with in life at the moment?

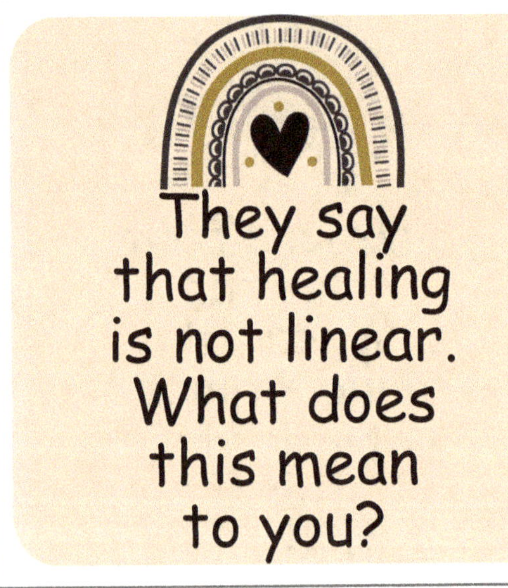
They say that healing is not linear. What does this mean to you?

Do you think your loved one is at peace right now?

Do you ever feel the presence of your loved one?

Do you believe in an after life?

Do you
dream
about your
loved one?

What advice
would you give
a friend that
had lost
a love done?

Do you have
a favorite place
that you like
to go and visit
your loved one?

Is there any
dates or events
that you find
harder than
others?

Do you like
to celebrate
their
birthday?

Do you think
it is important
to share your
feelings?

Little by little
we let go
of loss, but
never of
love.

How lucky
I am, having
some thing
that makes
saying goodbye,
so hard.
-Winnie the Pooh.

I can take
things one
day at
a time.

I am going
to try and
honour
my loved one
the best I can.

I'm allowed
to talk about
my grief,
I don't need
to hide it..

Grief is like
the wind, you
can feel it, but
you can't see
it.

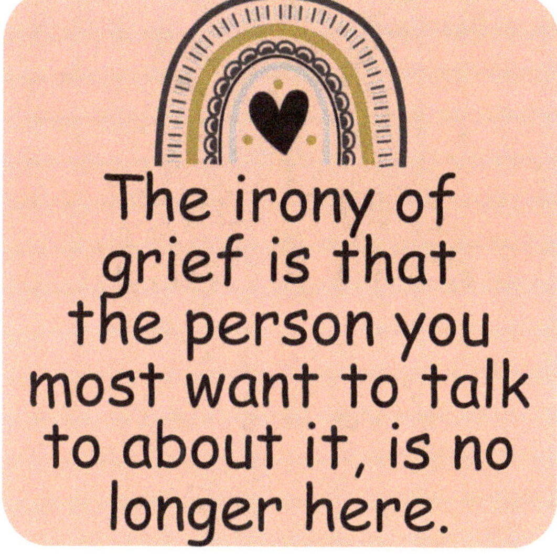

The irony of
grief is that
the person you
most want to talk
to about it, is no
longer here.

There is no
pain so great
as the memory
of joyin the
present grief.

In another
time,
in a happier
place,we will
meet again.

As long as
there is love
and memory,
there is no
true loss.

Those we love
don't go away,
they walk
beside us
everyday.

Death leaves
a heartache
no one can heal,
love leaves
a memory no
one can steal.

Some people get awkward around death, why do you think that is?

How would you like people to support you more?

Do you feel like you need closure? If so, what could help you get it?

Did you have a funeral or memorial service? Talk to me about that experience.

If you could see your loved one now, what do you think they would say to you?

What does hope for the future look like for you now?

You've done an amazing job working through this journal. Grief is never easy, and it takes a lot of courage to face your feelings, reflect on memories, and learn how to cope with such a difficult experience. Remember, there's no right or wrong way to grieve, and it's okay to have both good and bad days.

As you move forward, don't forget the strength you've shown in taking care of yourself and expressing your emotions. Keep using the coping skills you've discovered, and don't hesitate to reach out to others if you need support.

Most importantly, always remember that grief doesn't define you. You have the power to heal, grow, and continue creating new memories while still holding onto the love you have for the person you've lost.

You are never alone in this journey, and it's okay to feel whatever you feel. Take it one day at a time, and be proud of how far you've come.